CHINESE CHARACTERS

TITLES IN THE SERIES

Discovering China

CHINESE CHARACTERS

Nina Train Choa

Better Link Press

This book is edited and designed by the Editorial Committee of *Cultural China* series

Managing Directors: Wang Youbu, Xu Naiqing

Editorial Director: Wu Ying

Consulting Editors: Wang Yuanlu, Gu Weikang, Huang Sixian

Editors: Yang Xinci, Yang Xiaohe

Text by Nina Train Choa

Interior and Cover Design: Yuan Yinchang, Li Jing, Xia Wei

ISBN: 978-1-60220-107-1

Address any comments about *Discovering China: Chinese Characters* to:

Better Link Press

99 Park Ave

New York, NY 10016

USA

or

Shanghai Press and Publishing Development Company

F 7 Donghu Road, Shanghai, China (200031)

Email: comments_betterlinkpress@hotmail.com

Printed in China by Shenzhen Donnelley Printing Co., Ltd.

1 3 5 7 9 10 8 6 4 2

CONTENTS

PREFACE

CHINESE CHARACTERS CAN be both intriguing and baffling for a foreigner. The flexibility of their definitions and usage can be difficult for someone who is used to achieving a very specific meaning from a word, rather than conveying a broader idea or feeling. For an English speaker, this degree of flexibility can be frustrating. Our strict English grammar does not translate easily into Chinese in which words can be used interchangeably as different parts of speech, and context is everything. Furthermore, although it has been lost somewhat in recent generations, a sophisticated use of Chinese requires memorization of not just thousands of characters, but also of multiple character phrases—what we might call idioms. These will be as baffling to a non-Chinese speaker as if we said "an apple a day" to a foreigner with no further explanation. And yet to a native speaker they convey a very deep meaning, usually with a strong historical aspect as well as a contemporary sense.

Chinese etymology, like our own etymology, can be a source of revealing information regarding both history and culture. To understand how words have come to mean what they mean—by examining their roots and progress—is interesting whether it be from their Latin and Greek roots, or by finding what the original drawing or pictograph was for a certain character. The strong pictorial aspect of Chinese, though perhaps resulting in a less flexible development, is extremely revealing. The relatively unadulterated course of its linguistic history—compared to English certainly, where new words from foreign languages were absorbed constantly—can give a tremendous insight into the roots of China's ancient culture.

The words herein are a tiny representation that I found intriguing in some way. They often involve simple aspects of daily life in ancient China and are interesting, revealing, charming and occasionally playful. Most of them require little explanation beyond the original pictograph. I have given the pinyin or "alphabetization" of each word as well as the word's definition and a brief visual history of its background.

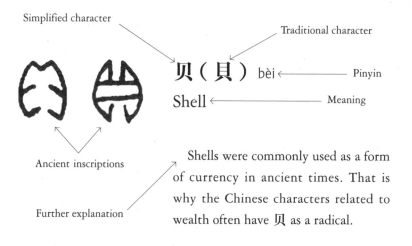

Simplified character

Traditional character

贝（貝） bèi ← Pinyin

Shell ← Meaning

Ancient inscriptions

Further explanation

Shells were commonly used as a form of currency in ancient times. That is why the Chinese characters related to wealth often have 贝 as a radical.

INTRODUCTION

O F THE SEVEN known forms of logosyllabic writing, Chinese is the only one that survives as a written language into the present day. Logosyllabic writing, which uses symbols to express words and phrases, has proven somewhat inflexible and difficult to adapt to increasingly complex linguistic needs. Logosyllabic writing existed as Sumerian in Mesopotamia, Prot-Elamite in Iran, Proto-Indic in the Indus Valley, Egyptian in Egypt, Cretan in Crete and Greece, and Hittite in Anatolia and Syria. Although some of these languages can still be found on archeological artifacts, China is the only place where the original logographic system developed the degree of sophistication necessary to survive as a viable form of communication. Although pronunciation varies throughout China, the written language, dating back more than 3000 years, is constant and has provided a strong historical connection for Chinese civilization and culture. Its remarkable age and strong visual element make it a critical and revealing part of Chinese culture.

In traditional etymology, Chinese characters are considered to have developed in six different but overlapping categories. These are called the "Six Categories". The first of these are pictographs; the next are ideographs; third are compound ideographs; fourth are meaning-phonetic characters; then characters which are assigned a new written form to better reflect a changed pronunciation; and the sixth are phonetic-borrowing characters. From a structural point of view, these can be examined as three basic categories.

The first category includes pictographs and ideographs. Pictographs include words like 日 (rì, sun), 月 (yuè, moon), and 鱼 (魚, yú, fish), in which a word is represented directly by a symbol—in the form of a graphic image. Slightly more complex, but still a pictograph, is the word 射 (shè, shoot), which combines a hand with a bow and arrow. The meaning of a pictograph tends to remain static and definite even if the depiction looses some of its resemblance to the original over time. The system is inherently limited as it requires the creation of a new picture for each thing or action represented and therefore becomes impractical as a language becomes more sophisticated. In some cases, abstract ideas are conveyed by ideographs. For instance where the idea is conveyed rather than an exact image. Examples of this are the numbers 一 (yī, one), 二 (èr, two), and 三 (sān, three), as well as words like 上 (shàng, above), and 下 (xià, below). Some of the original Chinese pictographs now form the skeleton of contemporary Chinese writing in the form of root characters or radicals. Radicals are used throughout Chinese as anchors for other more complex words. They serve to refer to a family of words. The radical gives an important clue to the meaning of the character in which it is found. For example, the characters for 语 (語, yǔ, language), 说 (説, shuō, talk), 讲 (講, jiǎng, speak), 讼 (訟, sòng, file a legal suit), 议 (議, yì, opinion) and 论 (論, lùn, discuss) all share the 讠 (言, yán) radical, which means each of these characters has a meaning related to language or talk.

The second category, meaning-phonetic characters, use two characters, one to convey meaning and one to indicate pronunciation. Any character can be used as a phonetic indication, but only a radical can be used as a determinative to convey meaning. Most Chinese words used today fall into this category. So for example, 梨 (lí, pear) and 犁 (lí, plow) both use the character 利 (lì, useful) to indicate pronunciation, but in the instance of 梨 (lí, pear) it is accompanied by the radical for 木 (mù, tree), for 犁 (lí, plow), with the radical for 牛 (níu, oxen).

The third category, phonetic-borrowing, grew from the need to expand on that basic system. The principle of phonetic-borrowing is to create a new word by "borrowing" from an ideograph with similar pronunciation. So, the character for 北 (north), pronounced "běi", is borrowed from the original character for 背 (back), also pronounced "bèi" —which was an ideograph of two people back to back 北. When this "borrowing" occurs, the original word must then be further refined to give it its original meaning again. Another example of this is the word 自 (zì) indicating self which borrowed the pictograph for nose 自 as a way of representing the self.

From a historical point of view, there are four principal periods in the history of written Chinese. The earliest period of Chinese writing dates from the Shang and Zhou dynasties and is referred to as the oracle bone inscriptions or *Jia Gu Wen*. These early markings are also known as shell and bone characters. Samples of this kind of writing date back to the period from about 1300 BC – 1000 BC and can be seen etched on ancient turtle shells and animal bones. Turtle shells were used for divination; the empty turtle shells were heated and the cracks created on the shell would be interpreted to predict the future. Inscribed ox bones were maintained as historical documents. The style of the characters from this period is very angular and practical. The next period sees the development of the bronze inscriptions or greater seal script, *Da Zhuan*. These characters mostly appear on cast bronze vessels between 1100 BC and 700 BC. This is followed by the lesser seal script or *Xiao Zhuan*. Initiated by Emperor Qin Shi Huang to unify the different writing scripts. The writing developed into an elegant flowing script which is more clearly the predecessor of the streamlined Chinese modern script. This script was frequently written on bamboo scrolls. The shapes and symbols which are in use today were developed during the end of Han dynasty, 206 BC to 220 AD, and are easier to use with both brushes and pens. Finally, China's standard script, known as *Kai Shu*, was introduced between 200 and 600 AD. In 1952, the Chinese developed and imposed the simplified version of

Chinese characters with fewer strokes per character which is in use all over mainland China today. Taiwan, Macau and Hongkong regions however still use the more complex traditional Chinese characters. There were more than 50,000 characters used during the Qing dynasty (1644 – 1911) compared to the present use of approximately 6,000. Today, knowledge of something like 4,000 characters is necessary to read a Chinese newspaper.

Radicals

This section covers characters directly to a symbol. They are often used as roots for other characters and are generally called radicals or root characters. Radicals form the skeleton of Chinese writing. They are often used as a base for other characters and refer to a family of words. Under each radical, a typical example is given, helping indicate the connection both between modern characters and their ancient forms.

贝（貝）bèi
Shell

Shells were commonly used as a form of currency in ancient China. Characters related to wealth often have 贝 as a radical.

贮（貯）zhù
To store

草 cǎo
Grass

Grass is a common radical in Chinese characters and used to make up many words related to plants.

叶（葉）yè
Leaves

册（冊）cè
Book

Before the invention of paper, Chinese was written on bamboo. Bamboo splints were strung together to make a book.

删（刪）shān
Delete

 车（車）chē
Car

This image is a plan of a moving vehicle. It appears in many characters related to locomotion.

军（軍）jūn

Army

火 huǒ
Fire

This is a graphic image which looks like something burning. It often used as a root or radical when a character has some relationship with fire.

炎 yán

Scorching

口 kǒu

Mouth

If a Chinese character has 口 as a root or radical, the character usually has some relationship with the mouth—speaking, eating, singing…etc.

吹 chuī

Blow

门（門）mén
Door, gate

A graphic image of an ancient Chinese door. It was traditionally made of two panels, often seen in characters related to opening and closing.

关（關）guān
Close

皿 mǐn
Utensil

In ancient China this radical was a generic term for all cooking and eating containers.

盆 pén

Basin
Tub

木 mù

Tree
Wood

In the oracle bone inscriptions and bronze inscriptions this radical means tree. Later it comes to mean wood and another character 树 (樹, shù) takes over the meaning of tree.

松 sōng

Pine
Soft

鸟（鳥） niǎo
Bird

Chinese characters related to aerial birds often have this avian image as a radical.

鸣（鳴） míng
Chirping of insects or small animals
Ringing

牛 níu
Ox, bull, cow

牛 is a generic term for ox, bull and cow.

牲 shēng

Domestic animal
Animal sacrifice

女 nǔ

Female, woman

In the oracle bone inscriptions and bronze inscriptions this radical looks like a woman kneeling with her hands crossed.

妹 mèi

Younger sister
Young girl

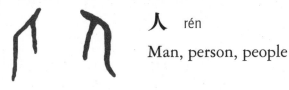

人 rén

Man, person, people

The radical 人 depicts a person in profile. In the oracle bone inscriptions and bronze inscriptions it appears in a great number of characters.

仔 zǎi

Son
Young man
Young animal

日 rì

Sun

If a Chinese character has 日 as a root or radical, the character usually has some relationship with time, weather, light or temperature.

晃 zé

Sun inclining to the west

山 shān

Mountain, hill

All Chinese characters with this root or radical are related to geology.

岳（嶽）yuè

High mountain

手 shǒu

Hand

We can see many characters made up by 手, meaning "to do". In oracle bone inscriptions and bronze inscriptions, this character can be facing either right or left.

播 bō

Sowing
Spread, broadcast

水 shuǐ

Water

This radical looks like running water and indicates that the word has some relationship with water.

浴 yù
Bath

丝（絲） sī
Silk

This image is the combination of two spindles. It relates to weaving, cloth, etc.

系 xì
Tie, fasten

 田 tián

Field, farmland

The 田 radical represents a field with an irrigation project. It appears frequently in characters relating to agriculture.

亩（畝）mǔ

Chinese unit of area equal

 网（網） wǎng

Net

A graphic image of a net.

罗（羅）luó

Net for catching birds
Collect, gather together

心 xīn

Heart
Mind

In ancient China, people believed that human beings used the heart to think, which is why characters related to thinking are often made up with 心 .

志 zhì

Will
Aspiration

 言 yán

Talk
Word To speak
To say

This is a pictograph of a tongue. Any Chinese character which has 言 (simplified 讠) as a root or radical, means to "say something".

许（許）xǔ

Praise or command
Allow or permit

 衣 yī

Clothes

You can see a collar and a sleeve in this image.

表 biǎo

Surface, outside
Show and express

鱼（魚）yú

Fish

This radical is a generic term for all kinds of fish.

鲜（鮮）xiān

Fresh and new
Delicious and tasty

雨（雨）yǔ
Rain

    In the oracle bone inscriptions and bronze inscriptions, this radical means "rain falling from clouds". All the Chinese characters with 雨 as a root or radical have some relationship with weather.

电（電）diàn
Electricity
Get or give an electric shock

月 yuè
Moon

Different from 日 (rì, sun), This is a half moon. In the oracle bone inscriptions and bronze inscriptions this character can be facing either right or left.

期 qī
Scheduled time
Period of time

舟 zhōu
Boat

A graphic image. As a radical it can make up characters meaning different kind of boats.

船 chuán

Ship

People or Body Parts

This section covers characters related to people or body parts. Images of hands, feet and heads as well as the whole body are used to create pictographs and ideograms. The most frequent radical to appear is 人 (rén), meaning person.

爱（愛）ài
Love

The original form of this character is two hands covering the heart. Later it combines four characters to suggest "love": a hand, the character for cover; a heart and the character for stop.

包 bāo

To wrap, include
A package, a bun

The original version of this character clearly depicts a baby inside its mother's womb. The meaning of wrapping and packaging is easy to extrapolate.

比 bǐ
To compare
Ratio, next to

The original character depicts two people next to each other facing right. The original meaning was "close", later it evolved to mean "compare".

Interestingly, in its oldest image, the character 从 (從, cóng), meaning "from" or "to follow", has two people standing very close, but facing left.

并 (並, bìng), like 比, shows two people facing left and joined by horizontal lines—meaning "togetherness".

斗 (鬥) dòu
To fight, exchange blows, wrestle

From its oracle bone inscriptions, this character looks like two men grabbing at each other's hair in a lively fight.

哥 gē
Older brother

One character for "brother" is directly below another identical character for "brother". The implication is that one older brother (below) is carrying the other younger brother above.

共（供）gòng
To offer
Together, sharing, common

Two hands can be seen here holding up a vessel. The idea of holding a vessel together original indicates offering something to ancestors. Then it develops the meaning "sharing", or having something in common.

鬼 guǐ
Ghost, soul of a man after death

The oracle bone inscription character shows a normal man's head, but with monstrously large eyes. The lower part of the body is also a normal shape. This distortion indicated that this was a person who has died and become a ghost. The character then developed the further meaning of cunning, mysterious and resourceful as ghosts were traditionally given these attributes.

Similarly, 异 (異, yì), meaning "strange" or "spooky" is a pictograph of two hands lifting to protect the head.

好 hǎo
Good, kind

The character for woman and child combine to make this character for "good". Not only are children a traditional source of happiness and prosperity, Chinese society also puts great emphasis on filial piety. Thus the image of a mother and child is full of positive associations.

化 huà
To change
Culture

This character consists of one person right side up next to another person—upside down—thus implying the same, but different...hence "change". It also implies people coming and going, which has a larger sense of associating with others and "culture".

欢（歡） huān
Happy

The character is made up of an image of an open mouth and the character for food. In a densely populated country visited by frequent famines it is easy to understand why food might come to be associated with happiness.

夹（夾）jiā

The space between things
Things made of two layers

Two smaller men can be seen in this character, one on each side of a large man being supported in the middle—indicating that they are supporting or helping him from the sides.

监（監）jiān

To scrutinize, supervise

The character is made up of a large eye, a person bent low looking down, and a vessel. The person is observing himself in the reflection made by the water in the vessel.

交 jiāo

To cross, intersect, associate with

交 depicts a man standing with his legs crossed lending itself to the idea of crossing and intersecting in a general sense.

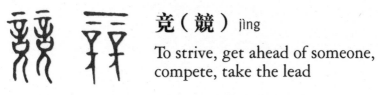

竞（競）jìng

To strive, get ahead of someone, compete, take the lead

The earliest versions of this character show two men running shoulder to shoulder; indicating a race or competition between them.

孔 kǒng

Hole, aperture, space

The character 孔 shows an infant sucking on a breast and gives the idea of aperture or opening.

曼 màn
Prolonged, graceful

The original character is of two hands holding an eye open. This implies "to look at something for longer", taking time—a "prolonged" look.

美 měi
Beautiful, beauty

A man wearing a feather head-dress can be seen in this character. The dress indicates that he is the decorated head of a tribe. This sense of "beautiful" can refer to talent and virtue as well as physical attributes. It can also be used to indicate the sweet and delicious taste of certain foods.

梦（夢）mèng
To dream

The original character of 梦 was made up of a man on top of a bed pointing to his eye—a very clear indication of what one "sees" when one is in bed. Later the character came to include the characters for eyebrow and for night.

民 mín
Common people, plebiscite

The original character is the shape of an eye being pricked by an awl. Historically, blinding in one eye was a form of torture inflicted on slaves or people being conquered.

Alternatively, the Chinese army also cut off the heads or ears of the vanquished. From this practice developed the character 取 (qǔ) meaning "to get" or "acquire", which, in the oracle bone script, was described by an ear being held in a hand.

母 mǔ
Mother

This character, which can also indicate "origin", is made up of the image of a person with exaggerated breasts in a kneeling position.

耐 nài
To tolerate, to bear

The character 耐, made up of a hand and a beard, refers to the traditional form of punishment of shaving off a man's beard for a lesser crime.

闹（鬧） nào
To make a loud noise, create a disturbance

A lesser seal ideograph which consists of

the character for market and the character for fight—giving a strong visual sense of noise and chaos.

妻 qī
Wife

Originally this character looked like a man grabbing hold of a woman's long hair. Presumably this is a reference to earlier, somewhat less formal times, when a wife would be abducted from a conquered tribe and taken by force.

Similarly, 奴 (nú), the character for "slave", depicted a hand grabbing a woman.

欠 qiàn

Lacking
To yawn, owe

In the oracle bone inscriptions this appears to be a man on his knees yawning. Characters with this radical have to do with exhaling: blow, sing, drinking. By implication, an absence of breath also came to mean a deficit or debt.

士 shì

Scholar-official, gentry
Soldier

In the early bronze inscriptions this character looks like an axe, a traditional symbol of power which would have been held by a warrior or person upholding the law. There is another differing theory that the image is in fact of a phallus, thus implying a man or person in power.

A related character is 父 (fù), meaning father. The bronze inscription version of this character looks like a hand holding an awl or axe. This was a weapon traditionally used to fight an enemy as well as to work in fields, and would have been held by adult males. This later developed the meaning of "father" specifically.

 叟 sōu
Old man

In the oracle bone inscriptions this character looks like a man holding a torch inside a room. This suggests needing light to look for something, or to search. Perhaps because of the decreased ability to see in the old, this came to mean old man.

Also related to the elderly, the character 老 (lǎo), meaning "old", is the image of a person with a walking stick.

太 tài

Greatest, too, over

Originally depicting one man placed over or above another man, this character implies "greater than" or great heights. Eventually the lower man came to be represented by a dot.

问（問） wèn

To ask

A mouth character can be seen between the two panels which make up the character for door. This suggests making an inquiry or asking a question.

显（顯） xiǎn

To show, display
Obvious

This character was originally a depiction of two long strands of hair in braids or plaits. The implication was to point out or display something—in this case with artifice and organization.

In a related character, 若 (ruò), meaning "similar" or "to seem", depicts a person coiffing his own hair with his two hands.

嚣（囂）xiāo
Arrogant, aggressive

This character is made up of four mouths and a head implying many people speaking at the same time.

孝 xiào
Filial piety

Filial piety was of immense importance in Chinese feudal society. This character depicts an old man being supported by a younger man; thus implying a father being supported and helped by his son.

休 xīu
To rest, stop

The character for person is placed next to the character for tree implying stopping under a tree or leaning on a tree for a pause while traveling or walking.

学（學） xué
To learn
Learning, theory, knowledge

This character 学 developed from an ideograph of a child arranging counting rods under a roof. These rods were normally used as an academic tool to study math.

有 yǒu

To have, possess, exist

The original character looks like an ox or perhaps a plant. These would indicate important possessions like livestock or a field. The later character looks like a hand holding a piece of meat; this implied both ownership and possession of an important asset.

自 zì

Self

The Chinese traditionally indicate themselves by pointing to their nose. This pictograph represents a nose and hence, "myself".

畧

果

Plants and Nature

This section is about words relating to plants and nature. Most of these characters have to do with the flora and fauna of everyday life. Many characters involve dogs, horses and other domestic animals and some use animals less present in everyday life, but important in other ways—like the tiger. Plants such as bamboo and rice are very common as are trees, which appear frequently in all forms—branches, roots, trunks. Many characters also developed from common celestial appearances: the sun, moon and stars.

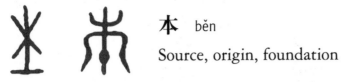

本 běn

Source, origin, foundation

A tree radical with a dot underneath to emphasize the root, serves to create the sense of "source". This character originally meant the root of the tree or the stem of a tree but later developed the meaning of "source" or "origin".

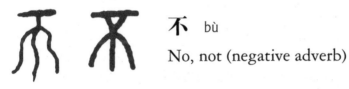

不 bù

No, not (negative adverb)

In the oracle bone inscription version of this character it has a horizontal stroke representing land, with a curving vertical stroke underneath representing roots or the embryo of a plant. The idea being that a plant over the ground exists fully, while the roots underground, still in an incipient state, are "not".

Similarly, the character 甫 (fǔ), meaning just or beginning, was originally depicted by a single seedling in a large field.

闯（闖）chuǎng

Rush, force one's way in or out, dash around madly

The character of a horse and a gate combine to give the idea of excitement and movement—a mad dash or rush.

春 chūn

Spring

The character 春 is inspired by the classic elements of spring: sun and the growing grass.

The other seasons are similarly depicted:

夏 (xià), summer, is an ideogram of a man with long naked hands and feet, giving the idea of hot weather.

秋 (qiū), autumn, is represented by the scene after a harvest. People set fire to the field to kill the pest.

Winter, 冬 (dōng), is made of a rope with a knot on each end, signifying the end of something, in this case the end of the year.

端 duān

Beginning, extremity

The character shows a seedling just breaking through the soil with its roots underneath. The horizontal line indicates the soil while the upper line refers to the budding plant above, creating the idea "of extremity" or "beginning".

A related character, 生 (shēng), meaning "to grow", depicts a seedling growing straight up on land.

奋 (奮) fèn

To lift oneself, to exert oneself, act vigorously

The lower character represents the ground while the upper character denotes a bird flapping its wings. Together they combine to give the idea of lifting and upward movement.

Another wing related character is 非 (fēi). Here wings are seen flapping in opposition. The meaning derived from this is "wrong" or "evil doing".

果 guǒ

Fruit
Result, outcome

In the oracle bone inscriptions, this character looked like a tree full of fruit—indicating the result of something, the outcome of effect or growth.

华（華）huá

Flourishing, prosperous

A flower and a plant radical combined to indicate prosperity.

Another character using flowers is 荣 (榮, róng), meaning "glory" and "honor", derived from the broader sense of flourishing and glorious. The character depicts a tree with many blooming flowers on its branches.

回 huí

Return, go back

The ancient form of 回 looked like a whirlpool and its meaning was closer to "circle" or "whirl". Eventually it came to be used more loosely with the general sense of "return".

集 jí

Gathering or assembly

In both the oracle bone inscriptions and the bronze inscriptions this character appears to be a bird perching in a tree. In the lesser seal characters this has become three bird parts denoting a group of birds perching together; a little group.

Another character related to birds is 噪 (zào), meaning "to chirp". The character is expressed by a tree with three mouths on the end of its branches.

骄（驕） jiāo

Proud, arrogant

The left character is a horse while the right

character is "lift high" which gives a vivid impression of a proud animal walking in an elegant and haughty manner.

解 jiě

To divide, separate, analyze, explain

In the oracle bone inscriptions this looks like two hands prying ox horns apart— dismembering the ox. This later developed the extended meaning of dividing, separating and analyzing.

晶 jīng

Bright and clear, Crystal

In the oracle bone inscriptions this appears as three stars. In the lesser seal script it has changed to three suns. Originally referring to a clear night, it has now developed the meaning of "bright" and "clear" in a more general sense.

昌 (chāng), meaning "exuberance", is represented by the character for sun, repeated twice.

明 (míng) however, also used to emphasize brightness and clarity, combines the character for both moon and sun.

  雷 léi
Thunder

The oldest form of this character shows lightning accompanied by four drum heads. Later, the rain radical was added above and the four drums were reduced to just one.

丽（麗）lì
Magnificent, beautiful

The oracle bone inscription and the bronze inscription versions of this character look like a deer with horns branching out prominently. Originally this character meant a pair or a couple and then developed the meaning "magnificent".

蒙 mēng
To cheat, dupe, deceive

The original character depicts hunters artfully covered in animal skins and horns disguising themselves from their prey. This has also been interpreted as animals covered by nets.

末 mò
End, tip, non-essential, minor detail
End

The character of a tree with a dot next to the top. The dot directs the attention to the smaller, less significant part of the tree, the tip or branch.

莫 mò

Not, without

In some ancient writing scripts this appears to be one sun part and four tree parts, implying that the sun is behind the tree or setting. The extended meaning came to be "without" or "not".

穆 mù

Solemn, quiet, harmonious

In the bronze inscriptions this character looks like a ripe rice plant with its heavy ears hanging down. The three dots nearby stand for the rice itself thus indicating a ripe crop. In a largely agricultural society, a ripe row of plants would be seen as a pleasant, harmonious image.

A related character, 来 (來, lái), meaning "to come", was originally depicted by a ripe wheat plant.

能 néng
Ability, talent, skill

The bronze inscription version looks like a bear—emphasizing its mouth, arched back, and claws. Bears are known for their strength and bravery and so the image came to represent various abilities and skills. This one having been "borrowed", the original character for bear was replaced with a new character.

虐 nüè
Cruel
Tyrannical

The lesser seal version of 虐 appears to be a tiger trying to capture or attack a man with his claws. The depiction of physical vigor and action is strong and the cruelty of the tiger can be imagined.

齐（齊）qí
Level, orderly, simultaneous

In the oracle bone inscriptions this looks like a line of wheat. The ears of wheat appear well lined up and in good order.

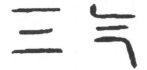

气（氣）qì
Air, gas, smell
Airs and manners, spirit, morale

The oracle bone inscription character is made up of three horizontal lines indicating floating clouds. The bronze inscription and lesser seal characters take on an even more cloud-like appearance. The character is also used to refer to a mood or temperament.

牵（牽）qiān

To lead along, pull, involve, implicate

The lesser seal character is made up of three parts—an ox, a nasal bolt and a string—thus giving the idea of leading along or pulling.

束 shù

To bind, control, restrain

The character of 束 depicts a bundle of firewood tied up and restrained in a faggot. This gives a clear idea of binding and restraining.

双（雙）shuāng

Two, twin, dual

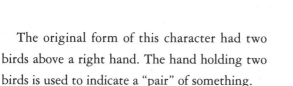

The original form of this character had two birds above a right hand. The hand holding two birds is used to indicate a "pair" of something.

突 tū

Suddenly
To rush forward, collide, break
through

The character, consisting of a dog and a hole
or gap, implies movement, speed and urgency as
the dog is emerging rapidly from the hole.

The character 霍 (huò), which means suddenly
or quickly, is made up of birds flying through
drops of rain. This implies speed and haste.

屯 tún

To store
Village

This character depicted a flower still in its bud giving the idea of something closed, protected or surrounded.

西 xī

West

Originally the character 西 was simply a bird's nest, with the bird being added later. This implies "west" as birds return to their nest in the evening, when the sun sets in the west.

昔 xī

Former times, the past

The oracle bone inscription character is clearly

a wave and a sun. This is believed to refer to the traditional Chinese belief that there had been a tremendous flood in ancient times during which people had to live high in the mountains to survive.

象 xiàng

Elephant
Likeness, image, scene

Both the oracle bone inscription and the bronze inscription characters are vivid sketches of an elephant in profile. As a pictograph, it is interesting that this character also came to be a reference to itself in its secondary meaning— that is: a likeness or image.

羞 xiū
Shame

The oldest form of this character is a sheep and a hand, implying a presentation or donation of mutton. This character was used to mean delicious, later it developed the meaning of "shame", as the present of a sheep was a means of making amends and so implies to make an apology.

嗅 xiù
To smell

The character for dog and the character for nose are combined to make reference to the canine's superior ability in this particular area.

衍 yǎn

To spread, broaden, develop

This character is made up of a river part and a movement part thus suggesting the water flowing through a river which can broaden as the river moves.

原(yuán), meaning "original" or "unprocessed" depicts a spring flowing down off the face of a cliff or mountain.

阳（陽） yáng

The masculine principle in Chinese philosophy
Sun, sunlight, anything protruding from a surface

The character 阳 has a phonetic compound

which originally referred to the south side of a mountain or north side of a river—the two sides which the sun reaches. In Chinese philosophy, the masculine is associated with the sun and the feminine with the moon.

晕（暈）yūn
Dizzy, giddy, faint

The oracle bone inscription shows a sun surrounded by dots in a circle. An ideograph, this character implies the dizziness and brightness felt from looking at the sun or being in the sun.

周 zhōu
To surround, twist
Circumference
A week

The oracle bone inscription character has a field part and four dots representing the crops, as well as movement, thus indicating farmland as opposed to wilderness or forest. It also indicates the cyclical aspect of farming. The character is also the name of a Zhou dynasty (c.1046 BC – c.221 BC) with roots in Shaanxi Province where agriculture was quite advanced. From field or farmland came the idea of perimeter or surround.

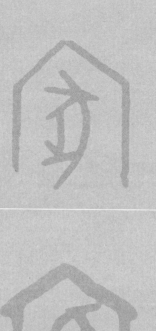

家

Objects

This section focuses on characters related to objects. Historically, the numerous objects relating to living, farming, cooking, animal husbandry, industry and social exchange would have been very familiar to everyone. They would have been an obvious source for a graphic shorthand. Even more specialized objects, for example those needed for producing silk or construction, as well as many musical instruments and weapons appear frequently in characters as they did in daily life.

安 ān

Peace, comfort
To be safe, to install

The original character depicts a woman sitting or kneeling alone in a room indicating peace and domesticity. In turbulent times of war or natural disaster, domestic tranquility was both prized and difficult to sustain.

备（備）bèi

To prepare
Provide

An early form of this character is an image of many arrows being placed inside a frame in preparation for shooting.

鄙 bǐ

Ignorant, vulgar, coarse
To despise, look down on

The oracle bone inscription character is made up of the characters for town and barn, and meant a "town" or "rural homestead". The bronze inscription character is similar but increasingly developed the more general meaning of remote or rural. In classic urban vs rural tradition, which still exists in China today, people from the country were considered less sophisticated than urban dwellers. In the Zhou dynasty (c.1046 BC – c.221 BC), 鄙 was used to refer specifically to a region with less than 500 families, stressing further the remoteness. Eventually the character came to indicate ignorant or less developed.

宾（賓）bīn

A visitor
To submit oneself to
(something or someone)

The oracle bone inscription character depicts

a man entering a room from outside. The bronze inscription character has an additional part representing a seashell next to the man. A seashell was a traditional gift or form of money and a visitor would have been expected to come bearing gifts.

卜 bǔ

To predict, estimate or select

In traditional Chinese geomancy, in order to answer questions about the future, a tortoise shell was baked and the ensuing cracks in the shell interpreted as predictions for the future. The character is reminiscent of the cracks formed on the back of a tortoise shell. This character is also said to be onomatopoeic, as the sound is like that of a turtle shell cracking.

常 cháng

Permanent or constant regulations

常 looks like the lower garment or skirt belonging to traditional Chinese costume. This traditional form of dress came to indicate something unchanging and fixed—a norm or tradition. From there it developed a more general meaning as a reference to permanent regulations.

典 diǎn

Classics, decrees and regulations
Standard works
Ceremony
To pawn

The oracle bone inscription original character looks like two hands holding a book. Books, being rare, would have implied a sense of something scholarly and official. In the later bronze inscription character, the book is on a table, but the meaning remains the same—a book in which laws and regulations are recorded. From there can be extrapolated the extended meaning of "responsibility" or "to be in charge".

对（對）duì
To adjust
Right, correct

This character has a somewhat architectural reference—the image depicts a hand erecting a pillar. The pillar has to be secured into a correct position to stay upright.

The character 直 (zhí) meaning "straight" or "vertical" was originally the juxtaposition of an image of an eye and a straight line.

福 fú
Good fortune, happiness

In the bronze inscription scripts, this pictographic character had a wine flask for the right character, while the left character represented an offering to ancestors. The Chinese traditionally sprinkled wine on the ground for good luck and as an offering.

妇（婦） fù
Wife or married woman
Woman

In both the oracle bone inscriptions and the later bronze inscriptions this character looks like a woman holding a broom. Only a woman with a home, a married woman, would have been in a position of responsibility for the housekeeping. Although certainly a position of subservience, this would also have been considered a position of responsibility, differentiating a married woman from a young girl.

富 fù
Rich, wealth, possessions
Abundant, plentiful

In the bronze inscription script, this character looks like a wine jar or vessel in a house. Having such a vessel in one's house would have been an indication of wealth and plentitude.

工 gōng

Work
Worker

The original form of 工 was a carpenter's square or perhaps a wood tamper or mallet—in any case a tool for a builder. From there it developed its larger meaning of "work" in a more general sense.

Similarly, in the oracle bone inscriptions, 专 (專, zhuān), meaning special or singular looks like a hand turning a spindle. The character, which originally meant spindle, has come to mean any specialty or skill.

和（龢） hé

Gentle, harmonious, mild
On friendly terms

The traditional character of 和 depicts bamboo pipes, a wind instrument on the left and a phonetic indicator on the right. Together they indicate a harmonious tune or lovely music. This in turn has come to mean harmonious in a more general sense.

轰（轟）hōng

A bang or boom
To rumble, to bombard or to explode
To shoo away or drive off

The original character was made up of three carts which, if moving together would certainly have made a great noise. This character is onomatopoeic—sounding like a great roar.

家 jiā

Household, family, home

The original character depicts a roof or structure with a pig inside. This represents a home or house where a family would have lived under one roof with their animals.

尽（盡）jìn

Finished, exhausted
Complete, to the limit

The oracle bone inscription version of this character looks like a man brushing a vessel with a bamboo branch held in his hand. Once emptied, a vessel would be cleaned; so the cleaning indicates that whatever was in the vessel has been exhausted or finished. The larger sense of "completion" developed by extension.

A similar idea can be seen in the character 扫（掃, sǎo) which means "to throw away" or "discard". This character is made up of a man holding a broom—perhaps sweeping.

开（開）kāi

To open, begin, unfold
To enlighten or remove obstacles

From the bronze inscription character and later developments, the character can be seen as two hands opening a door. The more conceptual meaning of "enlightenment" and "understanding", or "opening the mind", is extrapolated from the more literal meaning of "opening a door".

The character for door can be seen in a few other interesting characters: in 间 (間, jiān), meaning "the space in between" or "the middle", the image of the sun is slipping through the panels of a door.

客 kè

Guest
Customer, visitor

The character for 客 is created with the combination of the characters for house and arrive. The figure of a person can be made out standing in front of a house.

寇 kòu

Robber

To rob, invade

The oracle bone inscription character looks like a man being hit with a stick inside a house. Presumably the man has broken into the house and is being beaten off by the irate owner.

料 liào

To expect, predict or anticipate

This ideograph consists of the characters for rice and a measuring dipper. Rice was traditionally measured with a dipper, hence the meaning "to calculate" which later developed into the further meaning "to predict".

The character 兼 (jiān) also uses an image of rice. The meaning is "to combine" or "merge". The original character depicted a single hand grabbing two rice plants.

录（録）lù
Collection
To record, copy, employ

This character appears to be a hanging sack used for filtering wine. The sack was traditionally used to collect and then dispense the liquid slowly. The vertical lines at the bottom represent the liquid spilling out through the bottom of the sack.

乱（亂）luàn
A mess, disorder
Arbitrary

The character of 乱 originally depicted two hands arranging disheveled spools of silk, implying making order where there is disorder.

买（買）mǎi
To buy

The oldest form of this character is a representation of a net and a shell. Shells were commonly used as a form of money or for barter. They would be caught in a net and then used for financial transactions.

Similarly, the character 得 (dé) means "to obtain". It consists of a shell on the right and a hand on the left.

男 nán
Male, son

男 is made up of the characters for field and for plough. Agriculture being traditionally a man's work, it implied a son or male in the family or community.

器 qì
A utensil or instrument
Anything tangible and concrete—as opposed to abstract

The original character consists of four untensils surrounding a dog. Some scholars believe the four utensils are in fact mouths. The image implies a dog guarding something—or perhaps barking loudly. An ideograph, one can extrapolate how this became the representation for an actual, physical, "guardable" thing as opposed to an abstraction.

前 qián

To move forward
Before (in position or time)

前 is an ideograph which combines the characters for foot and for boat to imply forward movement and thus also "before" in a temporal sense. Some scholars believe the image is of two feet, one closely aligned behind the other.

实（實） shí

Solid, true, real, honest
Reality, fact

The bronze inscription version of this character is a house, a field and a shell. This would have been interpreted as wealth since owning land and shells (money) were signs of significant wealth. In the lesser seal characters the shell has become a string of coins.

我 wǒ
I, me

The oracle bone inscription version of this character was just a spear. In later versions it combines both spear and grain. These two things were deemed essentials for a definition of "self".

喜 xǐ
Happy, joyous
To like or celebrate

The oracle bone inscription character looks like a drum on a square frame surrounded by dots. The dots represent the sound produced by drumming. Beating drums was a traditional form of celebration. This character has also been interpreted as a bowl of food and a mouth signifying the pleasure and happiness of eating. Either way, the meaning is joyful and celebratory.

辛 xīn

Hot (in taste), bitter
Sad, hard

In the bronze inscription script this character looks like an instrument of torture, specifically like the instruments used to tattoo the faces of criminals; both to make them recognizable, and as a form of punishment. Extrapolated, this came to mean anything bitter, hard, or painful and from there also came to be used to describe hot or spicy food. Characters with this root always make reference to spiciness or torture.

新 xīn

New

The oracle bone inscription and the bronze inscription versions of this character both consist of wood and an axe in reference to the act of splitting wood. This meaning of chopping wood then developed further to mean something "new" as in freshly chopped wood.

益 yì

Abundant, rich
Benefit, profit, increase

The ancient form of this character showed a vessel overflowing with liquid, thus implying it had reached capacity and was full to the point of abundance. From this depiction of abundance can be extrapolated the extended meaning of "profit" or "benefit".

庸 yōng

Commonplace, mediocre

Traditionally, a classic Chinese palace or a city was surrounded by four gate towers. The character 庸, depicts that standard in architecture: four towers. It later developed the extended meaning of the "expected" or "commonplace".

至 *zhì*

To arrive, to reach
The most extreme point

In the oracle bone inscriptions this character looks very clearly like an arrow piercing the ground. The ground is represented by a horizontal line and the arrow is facing down. By extension this means "finality" and "arrival".

The character 人 (rù), meaning to enter or come in, is related—in this case the image is simply of an arrowhead.

The character 族 (zú) consists of an arrow as well as a flag. Here the meaning is clan, race or a class of similar things. The idea being that a clan or race would gather under a flag with their spears to go into battle.

三

气

BIBLIOGRAPHY

Chen Xianghui, *Chinese Characters in Pictures*. Sinolingua, Beijing, 2005

Lai, T.C., *Chinese Characters*. Swindon Book Company, Hong Kong, 1980

Shi Zhengyu, *Picture within a Picture*. New World Press, Beijing, 1997

Wang, H.Y., *The Origins of Chinese Characters*. Sinolunga, Beijing, 1993

Xie Guanghui, *The Composition of Common Chinese Characters*. Peking University Press, Beijing, 1997

Xiong Guoyin, *Ancient Chinese Characters in Pictures*. Qilu Press, Ji'nan, 2006

Zuo Min'an, *Expatiating on 1000 Chinese Characters*. Jiuzhou Press, Beijing, 2005

鱼

DYNASTIES IN CHINESE HISTORY

Xia Dynasty	2070 BC – 1600 BC
Shang Dynasty	1600 BC – 1046 BC
Zhou Dynasty	1046 BC – 256 BC
Western Zhou Dynasty	1046 BC – 771 BC
Eastern Zhou Dynasty	770 BC – 256 BC
Spring and Autumn Period	770 BC – 476 BC
Warring States Period	475 BC – 221 BC
Qin Dynasty	221 BC – 206 BC
Han Dynasty	206 BC – 220 AD
Western Han Dynasty	206 BC – 25 AD
Eastern Han Dynasty	25 AD – 220 AD
Three Kingdoms	220 AD – 280 AD
Wei	220 AD – 265 AD
Shu Han	221 AD – 263 AD
Wu	222 AD – 280 AD
Jin Dynasty	265AD – 420AD
Western Jin Dynasty	265 AD – 316 AD
Eastern Jin Dynasty	317 AD – 420 AD
Northern and Southern Dynasties	420 AD – 589 AD
Southern Dynasties	420 AD – 589 AD
Northern Dynasties	439 AD – 581 AD
Sui Dynasty	581 AD – 618 AD
Tang Dynasty	618 AD – 907 AD
Five Dynasties and Ten States	907 AD – 960 AD
Five Dynasties	907 AD – 960 AD
Ten States	902 AD – 979 AD
Song Dynasty	960 AD – 1279
Northern Song Dynasty	960 AD – 1127
Southern Song Dynasty	1127 – 1279
Liao Dynasty	916 AD – 1125
Jin Dynasty	1115 – 1234
Xixia Dynasty	1038 – 1227
Yuan Dynasty	1279 – 1368
Ming Dynasty	1368 – 1644
Qing Dynasty	1644 – 1911

水

INDEX